Dedicated to
Ryan, Jeremy, Nathan
and all of the athletes at Elite Camps.

Text & illustration copyright © 2024 by Stephanie Rudnick. All rights reserved.

Rookie Baller by Stephanie Rudnick.

Published by Sport Lessons Press

www.elitecamps.com

No part of this publication may be reproduced in whole or in part, or stored in a retrieval system, or transmitted in any form or by any means, electronic, mechanical, photocopying, recording, or otherwise, without written permission of the publisher/ author.

For information regarding permission, write to steph@elitecamps.com

ISBN: 978-0-9958984-1-7

In the sunny town of Hoopville,

lived a happy basketball player named

Rookie Baller.

Rookie Baller loved playing basketball

with his buddies.

At his first school game, Rookie Baller felt butterflies in his tummy.

Oops! He tried to dribble, and the ball hit his foot. His friends giggled.

Rookie Baller blushed and felt a little blue.

Coach Swish saw Rookie Baller looking gloomy.

He said, 'Dribbling takes lots of practice, Rookie Baller.

All great players mess up sometimes, but they don't stop trying.

Mistakes help us learn and grow!'

Rookie Baller practiced every single day.

He dribbled on his driveway.

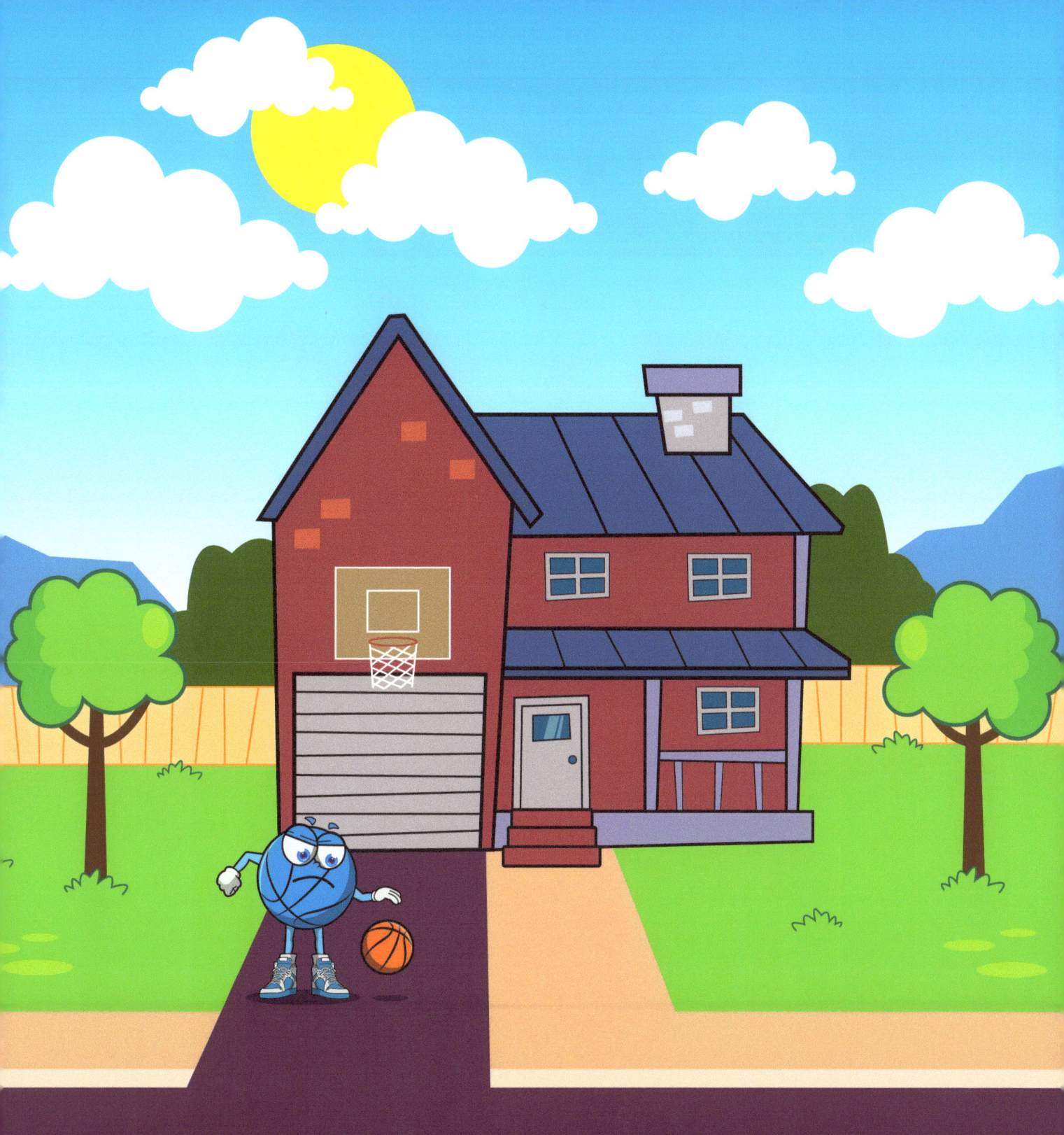

He dribbled on his way to school.

He even dribbled in his basement.

At first, it was tough for Rookie Baller.

But he kept smiling, even when the ball hit his toe.

He remembered Coach Swish's words:

'Mistakes are how we learn.'

Slowly, Rookie Baller got better at dribbling!

His friends saw that the ball didn't hit

his foot anymore on his way to school.

At the next game, Rookie Baller was a bit nervous but thought of all his practice.

This time, Rookie Baller dribbled smoothly across the court!

His friends cheered as he made a shot.

Rookie Baller still lost the ball sometimes.

But he remembered, 'Mistakes are part of learning,' just like Coach Swish said.

After the game,

Coach Swish said, 'You were amazing, Rookie Baller! Your practice really showed.'

Rookie Baller kept practicing his dribbling.

He even taught other little players.

He helped them see that making mistakes helps us get better.

In Hoopville,

everyone learned from Rookie Baller that

with practice, you can get better at anything!

Questions To Ask Your Child After Reading The Book

Have you ever felt nervous like Rookie Baller when you try something new?

What is something you practice to get better at, just like Rookie Baller practiced basketball?

How do you feel when you make a mistake? Do you think it's okay to make mistakes?

Can you think of a time when you kept trying even though something was hard?

What would you say to a friend who is feeling sad about not being good at something?

About The Author

Stephanie Rudnick is a mother, a writer, a motivational speaker, and the founding owner of Elite Camps, one of the largest basketball organizations of its kind in Canada, serving 6,000 athletes annually.

Stephanie's passion for basketball is stronger than ever.

Once a high-level player, she now helps athletes develop their on-court skills while ensuring that they, their parents, and their coaches all understand how the lessons learned on-court can prepare them for success in life.

Stephanie lives in Ontario with her husband, David, and their three sons.

www.elitecamps.com

A Word By The Author

If you enjoyed this book, it would be wonderful if you could take a moment to leave a lovely review on Amazon, as your kind feedback is very appreciated and so very important to help spread the word about books designed to support families on their sports journey. Thank you so very much for your time.

Click this link to leave a review

https://linktr.ee/stephanierudnick

www.ingramcontent.com/pod-product-compliance
Lightning Source LLC
Chambersburg PA
CBHW041437010526
44118CB00002B/102